# DOES YOUR RESUME MAKE YOUR PHONE RING?

*Executive Coach Reveals*

*Job Searching SECRETS Employer's*

*Don't Want You to Know.*

Volume 4, 1st Edition

To

*THE CAREER POTENTIAL SERIES*

By

# EDWARD J. MURPHY

CAREER MAKER PUBLISHING

## *WHAT OTHERS SAY ABOUT*
## *EDWARD J. MURPHY*

*"I thought I could write a wonderful resume until I had your assistance in preparing a better resume to replace it. I thought I knew how to find a position with a company until you showed me 19 ways to do it. I thought I could handle almost any question until you showed me how wrong I was. I thought I did not need any job interview role-play exercises until you critiqued the results of my videotaped interview. Luck is when preparation meets opportunity. You prepared me and gave me the opportunity to prove my worth to a company. That means you are my luck."*

*- Roy P., Bellevue, WA*

*"Ed was tremendously instrumental in directing and assisting the implementation of my career search. It was through his dogged persistence, guidance and genuine encouragement that kept me on track and lead me to the successful position of receiving multiple offers accepting an offer from ...corporation. This was all done in 60 days. Ed was always available when I needed clarification of what I was doing, with recommendations and suggestions as to how to maximize my efforts."*

*- Jim S. Rancho Santa Fe, CA*

*"I have appreciated your candor, inspiration, insight and practical experience. I have found your goal identification exercises, negotiation skills, and personal growth strategies particularly useful both personally and professionally. I would most heartily recommend your services as a personal coach to anyone who has high moral character, is intrinsically motivated, and has a desire to be the best they can be."*

*- Cliff J., Kansas City, MO*

## DEDICATION

---

I DEDICATE THIS BOOK

TO

My *Soul-Mate and Wife,*

# *DIANA K. PETERSON-MURPHY*

*Diana saved me just in the nick-of-time. After meeting Diana, my life keeps getting better. She is my eternal, soul-mate. She taught me how to overcome my fear.*

# TABLE OF CONTENTS

# INTRODUCTION

---

*"Keep interested in your career, however humble; it is a*
*real possession in the changing fortunes of time.*
*- Desiderata*

What's the purpose of your resume? I'll bet you think the purpose of your resume is to get a job, right? Wrong! This could not be farther from the truth.

The purpose of your resume is to make your phone ring, period!

This is the ultimate test of your resume; if your phone doesn't ring, your resume is worthless.

Your phone isn't ringing because your resume is not compelling enough for someone to call. Your resume isn't compelling enough because it doesn't speak in the language every employer speaks; Employer Speak.

After reading this book you'll learn *Employer Speak* and be able to modify your current resume into a compelling resume that will make your phone ring for job interviews.

I know from experience, that there's nothing more stressful than trying to conduct a job search - after losing your job. I've been there!

*It's a SCARY time!*

You have no cash flow and you're surviving on savings and help from friends and family. The fear and uncertainty of when you'll be reemployed are crushing on you and your family.

The biggest frustration is the Silence; your phone never rings - even after weeks and months of effort.

You've done everything you know how to do and nothing so far has worked. The fear of the unknown, the embarrassment, the lack of self-worth and self-doubt are mounting. You're desperate and ready to take any job just to support your family.

How much longer can you continue your insane behavior; doing the same thing over and over again, while expecting a different result? There must be a better way!

Well there is and it's time for a change – this is why I wrote this book. I can help you!

One of my clients said it best when he wrote,

*"Thanks to Ed, I learned the secrets of running a successful job search and in only two weeks I found my career position. I actually had two offers from which to choose and was able to leverage that situation into a 10% raise plus a bonus, all before I ever worked a day. Thanks doesn't seem enough."* – William S., San Diego, CA

I bring over 21 years of experience as an Executive Coach, helping hundreds of people, from recent college graduates to CEO's, find meaningful employment. I worked for four of the largest consulting, outplacement and e-cruiting companies in America in Seattle, San Diego, and Kansas City.

It was here that I learned the Secrets of making my client's phone ring.

### Without a phone call – your search is dead!

To make your phone ring you'll need a compelling resume; one that speaks in a language every employer understands and sells your potential.

This book is unique because it:

- Teaches the SECRET language only employers speak
- Reveals how to make your resume more compelling
- Comes from my personal struggles finding employment and the struggles of my clients over a 15-year period
- Teaches you specifically what employers are looking for
- Helps you think and speak in a language every employer understands
- Includes all the things you want to know and the top things you didn't realize you needed to know
- And, much, much, more!

Everything in this book has worked for me, worked for my clients, and I know they'll work for you!

One thing I know for certain, sitting home and waiting for your phone to ring, is the definition of complacency, which will kill your job search and your career.

*Stop wishing you were better and do something about it today!*

Also, if you feel this information could help someone else, please take a few moments to let them know. If it turns out to make a difference in their life, they'll be forever grateful to you – as will I.

*Let's make a difference together - one person at a time!*

All the best!

*Ed*

Founder of TheCAREERMaker.com

*email: ed.murphy77@gmail.com*

---

**Note:** Marked in **Segoe Print** throughout this book, you'll find *Takeaways* or *Key Points* which summarize the main message we wish to convey.

*You're not just looking for a job, you're looking for a place for your CAREER to happen.*

# CHAPTER 1:
# WHAT LANGUAGE DO EMPLOYER'S SPEAK?

*"The things that matter most should never be at the
mercy of the things that matter least."*
*-Johann Wolfgang von Goethe*

Have you ever struggled trying to determine what's most important and what's not; especially when there are too many things to do and too few people and hours in the day to get it all done?

To survive requires focus and prioritization. Many new employers let their employer decide what's most important because they fear making a mistake. However, small business owners, entrepreneurs, and consultants don't have this luxury. Here's a methodology to help ensure your focus and priorities are clear to help you survive.

Here, we'll be examining both Private Sector Corporations like Microsoft and Public Sector Organizations like School Districts and Government Agencies, to better understand what's most important to their survival.

## What matters most to the survival of
## *PRIVATE SECTOR CORPORATIONS?*

Have you ever struggled trying to figure out what matters most? If not, you will. Especially, when there are too many things to do and too few people and hours in the day to get it all done. Well, it all comes down to Focus and Priority. But how can you focus or prioritize without knowing what matters most? This is why we'll be examining Private Sector Corporations like Microsoft to better understand what matters most to their survival.

As an Executive Coach, I often asked senior executives from Private Sector Companies, "What matters most to the survival of your company?" The first answer I normally got was People. And, people are an important resource, but not the most important resource. Just quit your job and see how quickly you'll be replaced. Some said Technology, which is important, but again, not the most important. So, what really matters most? The only people who don't struggle with this question are Small Business Owners. These guys get it.

*Any small business owner will tell you that the correct answer is Positive Cash Flow (or PCF).*

Without PCF, the company can't pay their bills and they're soon out-of-business. Without PCF, the company's bankrupt. Game over! And, according to the Small Business Administration, this is the primary reason why 80% of start-up companies fail within their first 3 years. But what about your business unit? If you can link what you and your business unit do for your company's PCF and how it has improved or achieved better results, your business unit is essential to your company.

In the same vein, if your business unit can't be directly linked to one or more of the activities that generate PCF, your unit could be considered non-essential and therefore expendable - not a place you want to stay for long. So, what activities generate *Positive Cash Flow*?

### *What Generates PCF?*

Here are the four most important activities that generate Positive Cash Flow for Private Sector companies like Microsoft:

- **Increase Revenues:** To increase revenues from the sale of products and services normally involves those in sales, marketing, sales support, business development, or strategic development. Can you find and recommend new and innovative ways to sell more products or services like any of these activities? Bringing in new customers, selling more to the same customers, discovering new uses for old products, or finding new ways to bring more money in the door, are how revenues are increased.

- **Decrease Operating Costs:** Decreasing operating costs, or saving money, is everyone's job. Can you find and recommend new and innovative ways to reduce costs like any of these activities: consolidating, eliminating, cost sharing, getting a better price from a supplier, conserving, saving time or being more effective, efficient, and consistent? Because this is how Operating Costs are decreased.

- **Better Use of Available Resources:** Everyone's job is to better use the resources they already have. Can you find and recommend new and innovative ways to better use the resources your company already has like any of these activities: streamlining, eliminating redundancies, consolidating, conserving, waste reduction, process improvement, reducing time required, becoming more efficient, doing more with less, better maintaining equipment and vehicles to extend their service life and finding quicker or easier ways of doing things. And how much money or time could be saved annually? Because this is how to better use the resources of your company.

- **Anticipate Problems Today to Save Money Tomorrow:** Anticipating problems today to save money tomorrow is also everyone's job. Since law suits are very expensive, can you find and recommend new and innovative ways to anticipate problems today to save money tomorrow like any of these activities: creating important policies and procedures, creating better contracts, ensuring the right insurance is in force, ensuring compliance with outside agencies, creating better physical and cyber security procedures, creating better property accountability procedures, or eliminating unsafe conditions. This is what saves money tomorrow by anticipating problems today.

### How can you best use this knowledge?

If you work for a Private Sector Company like Microsoft, your career depends on your ability to identify, measure, and increase your value added (individual productivity and sustainability) to one or more of the four activities that contribute to PCF.

This step only pertains to half the Job Market. What about all those who are not profit driven like nurses, teachers, fireman, and all those who put themselves in harm's way every day to defend us and keep us safe? Not every organization is profit driven. So, how do they identify, measure and increase their value add?

## *What matters most to the survival of*
## *PUBLIC SECTOR ORGANIZATIONS?*

Since these organizations do not focus on profit generation, what matters most to them is providing a service that serves the greater good (like schools and government agencies).

*Public Sector Organizations use what is called a Band Of Excellence (BOE) to measure and assess their level of services.*

For those who work in the Public Sector, like teachers or government workers, they are required to achieve, maintain, or exceed the *Band Of Excellence (BOE)* set by their organization. So, what is a *Band Of Excellence?*

**Band Of Excellence:**

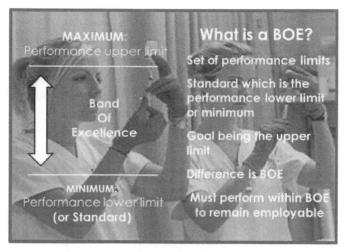

A *Band Of Excellence (BOE)* is a set of performance limits ranging from the Minimum (The Standard) - being the performance lower limit and the Maximum - being the performance upper limit. And the difference between the Minimum and the Maximum is called the *Band Of Excellence*. If your performance stays within the *Band Of Excellence*, you remain employable.

And, here's a simple example.

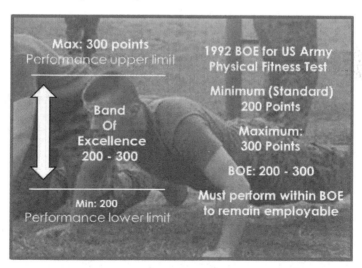

The biggest government agency on the planet is the US Department of Defense. In 1992, as a former US Army Officer, here's the BOE all soldiers used when taking the 5 event, Annual Physical Fitness Test.

The BOE Minimum (or Standard) was 200 points overall. The BOE Maximum was 300 points overall. The BOE was 200 - 300 for the test overall to remain promotable. If a Soldier failed to achieve 200 points overall, he was retrained and re-tested. If he failed a second time, he was considered un-promotable and administratively processed for release from the military.

### How does this apply to the Business World?

Let's take teachers and government workers as an example. To remain employable, they're continuously assessed by their supervisors using assessment standards for specific job tasks and behaviors. Employers use these activities to assess both individual and unit performance against their BOEs.

Public Sector BOEs are measured by daily observations, customer feedback, certification, performance reviews, external audits, visits, compliance inspections, annual qualification, and even continuing education.

### How is Performance Measured?

BOE's are used to measure and assess both individual and unit performance, which includes results, behavior, and potential. If each follower continues to meet their BOE Standards, they remain employable. If not, they are retrained, retested and either put on probation, reinstated, or released. And, if they achieve, maintain, or exceed their BOE Maximums, they should expect some form of recognition.

BOE's are needed to measure excellence in Public Sector Organizations because they're not driven by Positive Cash Flow. They are used to make periodic assessments to determine if individuals, units, and systems have achieved, maintained, or exceeded their BOEs. Without a BOE, you can't measure performance or even tell if you're improving or getting worse.

*BOEs are also used by Private Sector Corporations to help generate Positive Cash Flow.*

**How are BOEs Created?**

To create any Public Sector Organization, it must go through these three phases:

Phase 1: Must serve the greater good (schools or government agencies)

Phase 2: Must create a BOE to maintain or enhance that service

Phase 3: Must consistently achieve, maintain, or exceed their BOE

This is how they maintain the funding needed to operate, which comes from city, state, and federal tax revenues. And, if the organization can no longer meet their BOE Standards for services, they run the risk of losing their funding.

*If you work for a Public Sector Organization, like school districts or government agencies, your career depends on your ability to identify, measure, and increase your BOE value added.*

Summary: The two things every company in the world must have to survive:

- *Private Sector Companies* (like Microsoft and all other For Profit Companies) must generate PCF and achieve, maintain, or exceed their BOEs.

- *Public Sector Organizations* (like School Districts) must achieve, maintain, or exceed their BOEs and receive external funding.

*Employer's think and speak PCF/BOE.*
*It's that simple-don't screw it up!*

# CHAPTER 2:
# WHAT VALUE DO YOU BRING TO AN EMPLOYER?

*"Price is what you pay. Value is what you get."*
*- Warren Buffett*

Now that you know that employers speak and think PCF/BOE, how can you make your resume speak PCF/BOE? To figure that out, let's first identify your "value added".

To identify your *value added,* here are the most important questions to ask to determine how you're linked to PCF/BOE. Answering these questions will help you determine how you (and your business unit) are linked to the things that matter most: contributing to your Leader's PCF/BOE goals. So, let's review each, one at a time.

**How do you contribute to your Leader's PCF/BOE goals?**

Here's a true story.

> *One day, Bob was called for a job interview for a job that he really wanted. This new job came with a promotion and doubled his salary. You know the drill; this is where you get the opportunity to justify your existence to complete strangers.*

*As expected, Bob was nervous, especially when the interviewer started out by asking him, "Why should we hire you?*

*After Bob picked himself up off the floor, he stammered something that most people would say, "Well, I was responsible for...."*

*Then, to make things worse, the interviewer interrupted him and said, "Stop! No one cares what you were responsible for. I want to know what you achieved. What got better because you were there? What was your value added (individual productivity and sustainability) to your leader?"*

Unfortunately, Bob didn't get the job, which was a shame because he was the best of all of those they interviewed.

*He just didn't know his value added.*
*Bob didn't know how to sell himself.*

This story unfortunately is the norm rather than the exception. All too often good people have no clue what's most important to a potential leader or how to articulate their value added. Has this ever happened to you? If not, it will. But, by reading this guide, you'll never hesitate to answer these questions.

Your value added is quite simply the sum of everything you bring to the table (like your knowledge, skills, experience, achievements, attitude, relationships, character, and balance) that has contributed, in some measurable and significant way, to the achievement of your leader's goals.

You already know how important it is to your career to be able to add value to your leader. But, did you know that most people have no clue how to do that. The problem comes from the fact that few people truly understand what matters most to the survival of their organization.

*Once you learn how to identify, measure and increase your value added to your leader, you're well on the way to becoming absolutely essential.*

Most people only begin to identify their value added near the end of their career, if at all. To identify your value added (individual productivity and sustainability), here are the most important questions to ask to determine how you're linked to PCF/BOE. Answering these questions will help you determine how you (and your business unit) are linked to the things that matter most: contributing to your leader's PCF/BOE goals. So, let's review each one.

### How do you contribute to your Leader's PCF/BOE Goals?

It all starts out with a few assumptions. The first assumption is that you know your leader's goals. If not, ask. Second assumption is that your leader's goals are measurable. And the third assumption is that you (or your unit) contribute directly to your leader's PCF/BOE goals.

### What do you (or your business unit) do (what duties do you perform)?

Are your duties essential to the survival of your company? How do you help others and who are you helping? What are you doing to better help others? Most followers don't deal directly with customers. Most often, your #1 customer will be another follower or unit within your company.

### What are your PCF/BOE Standards to achieve, maintain, or exceed?

What's the *Band of Excellence?* How do you contribute to your leader's PCF/BOE Goals? Standards here mean the minimum acceptable level of performance (results and behavior). This includes the stated, inherent, and expected standards for the duties you perform. Where's the line between the acceptable and unacceptable? What does your leader and organization expect of your performance (results and behavior)?

### How does your Leader measure this?

How does your leader measure your performance (results and behavior)? Who does the measuring? What are the metrics and how often does your leader make assessments?

### How does your performance compare to your peers?

Compare to your peers means compare yourself to those at your level within your organization. What are they doing to become better? While this is not the best method for comparison, it's important to collaborate with your peers - because you'll learn a lot.

### How does your performance compare to a year ago?

*The best way to measure your performance is to compare yourself to where you were a year ago.*

### Are you getting better over time?

Are you getting better or worse? How do you know for sure? Who is counting or measuring? What are the metrics? If so, how much better? Without measuring and keeping track of how you're doing, how can you ever answer this question?

### What do you get for being the best or for improving?

Are there incentives in place for continuous excellent performance? Have you received awards, promotions, raises, accolades, kudos, or other recognition? Do you have copies of this recognition? What was the recognition for? What did you do to earn it?

*If you're not improving, guess what your peers are doing?*

This also includes professional development, which means additional education, training, and certifications.

### What improved because you were there?

From the first day you started, until today, what have you done or recommended to be done that got better because you were there? What was your contribution to moving the work forward? What have you done to make your performance more effective, efficient, and consistent?

*Answering these questions will help you determine how you (and your unit) are linked to the things that matter most: your leader's PCF/BOE goals.*

# CHAPTER 3:
# WHAT ARE YOUR ASSETS AND LIABILITIES?

*"I have no particular talent. I am merely inquisitive."*
*– Albert Einstein*

Before learning how to identify your assets and liabilities, it's important to understand a few important warnings.

**Warning #1:** Don't quit your job unless you have a guaranteed better job to move too. If you quit, you lose two valuable things; unemployment insurance and severance.

**Warning #2:** Don't fall into the trap of waiting until your unemployment insurance and/or severance runs out before starting your search. It could take you at least one-month for each $10,000 in the pay you're seeking before you find a new position, or longer. Always be looking for a better opportunity even after you become reemployed!

**Warning #3:** Don't take your foot off the job search accelerator! Just because one opportunity looks good, don't slow down your search. At the last minute, this good opportunity could disappear and you'll be left with nothing, feeling demoralized. Don't stop your search actions until the day after your first day at your new job.

## *Identify your Assets*

Let's take an inventory of your assets. Your assets are your knowledge, skills, experience, attitude, achievements, relationships, and balance. This is what you bring to the table. This is what you're selling - your potential!

Here are the Asset Categories:

- <u>Knowledge:</u> What knowledge do you have? Have you been tested and found worthy? What is your level of educational, certification, license, and special training?

- <u>Skills:</u> What can you do with your knowledge? What're your transferrable skills? What can you do to enhance your employer's results?

- <u>Experience:</u> What different environments (locations, industries, sectors, level, functional areas, size of company, Fortune 1000 companies) have you been in and how long?

- <u>Achievements:</u> How well did you (or your team) perform? What did you accomplish? What got better because you were there? How did it improve your employer's results? What obstacles did you overcome?

- <u>Character:</u> How do you treat others? True character is right behavior; what you say and do when no one's around including traits like Adaptable, Dependable, Integrity, Judgment, Loyalty, Moral Courage, Positive Attitude, Drive and Respect.

- <u>Relationships:</u> How well do you work with others? What would others say about your people skills? Have you ever led a team? What drives you crazy? What's important in your relationship with your Leader? Who do you know that can help us?

- <u>Balance:</u> How balanced is your life overall? Is there anything in your life that is out of balance that could become a distraction to your career later? If you're out of balance, this could be a liability.

### *This is what you're selling - so make it count!*

Your job during the interview is to increase the perceived value of your assets. Your assets are what produce results for the employer lucky enough to have you on their team.

## *Identify your Liabilities*

Social networking (LinkedIn, Facebook, and Twitter could be a liability. 50% of employers admit checking social networking sites before making a hiring decision. Because of this, don't post information concerning politics, religion, sex, or humor (includes content and photos). If they're already there, remove them!

Other liabilities include:

- No GED, High School, or College
- No training in the industry
- No computer skills
- No experience in the industry or function
- Appearance: Poor hygiene, overweight, smoker, poor health
- Bad credit, criminal record (Felony DUI)
- Age: Too old or too young; Lack of experience
- Inability to communicate your transferable skills
- Over qualified (too much education and/or experience)
- Being out of work too long, gaps in your resume
- Been in three companies in the past five years
- Bad performance reviews
- Lack of good references

As you assess your liabilities, prepare to respond to each during an interview.

*Being prepared is vital to your success.*

# CHAPTER 4:
# WHAT'S YOUR SEARCH FOCUS?

*"Don't be afraid to give your best to what seemingly are small jobs. Every time you conquer one it makes you that much stronger. If you do the little jobs well, the big ones will tend to take care of themselves."*
*- Dale Carnegie*

Your search focus is critically important. Without it, you'll just be a wandering generality.

### How do Employers Fill Vacancies?

Because time is critical, employers normally fill vacant positions by;

- *Selecting someone from within their company*

- *Asking for referrals from their employees*

- *Asking for referrals from family, friends, and associates*

- And, as a last resort, they create a job requisition (including the duties and responsibilities, minimum prerequisites, and desired skills) to begin the hiring process which could take several weeks (if not months)

Special Note: Notice that many positions are filled from referrals from others. These positions won't be advertised. This is important because it shapes your actions during your search! You can only access them by using the techniques presented in this guide.

## How do People Find Jobs?

Most people find jobs through word of mouth referrals and by contacting companies directly. However, all these sources produce results.

- ***Word of mouth - 35%***

- ***Contacting companies - 30%***

- Ads and internet - 14%

- Agencies and recruiters - 11%

- Referrals from schools, unions, trade journals, and civil services tests – 10%

Special Note: Notice that **65% of positions** come from word of mouth and contacting companies. These positions won't be advertised. This is important because it shapes your actions during your search! You can ONLY access them by using the techniques presented in this guide.

## What's the Role of Human Resources?

When applying for a posted job your resume will go directly to the Human Resources (HR) Office. This process could generate hundreds, if not thousands, of resumes. HR will screen all the resumes and select a few to send to a hiring manager. If the hiring manager likes what he sees, he will ask HR to schedule an interview.

This is the traditional hiring process (if the hiring manager can't find a replacement through referrals). As a result, this traditional process doesn't put the odds in your favor. You need a better way of getting your resume in front of the right people. This is why I wrote this guide.

To create your search focus, let's first create your 30-Second Commercial.

## *What's your 30-Second Commercial?*

*Your 30-Second Commercial is nothing more than
your answer to the question, "What do you do?"*

How do most unemployed people answer this question? Most people would say, Well, I've been laid off, fired, or downsized, or I'm doing some free-lance work, or I'm between positions, or whatever.

That kind of answer is not only bad self-talk, but it causes the person you're speaking to - to want to change the subject. So why put yourself in that awkward position. Instead, give a quick overview of your career by telling them how you've helped other people.

Your 30-Second Commercial should answer these questions:

- How do you see yourself (Title/Function)? I've been the…

- What have you done to improve business?

- How much experience do you have in which industries?

- What are you seeking?

When you practice your 30-second commercial in the mirror daily, ask yourself if the person in the mirror is articulate, enthusiastic and focused? If not, keep doing it until you are. This will prepare you for game-time, when you get to do it for real.

*Remember: your potential is the product you're selling.
Make your 30-Second Commercial count.*

**Sample 30-Second Commercial for someone who is UNEMPLOYED:**

*I've been the Director of Finance for several Fortune 500 companies in the Seattle and Kansas City area, where I managed a division of 45 associates. I helped save my employer $1.5 million recently converting our accounting functions over to a state-of-the-art software operation. I've spent the last 15+ years in the high technology manufacturing industry. I'm currently on an active search for a senior financial opportunity here in Kansas City.*

**Sample 30-Second Commercial for someone who is EMPLOYED:**

*I'm the Director of Finance for a Fortune 500 company here in the Kansas City area, where I manage a division of 45 associates. I recently save my employer $1.5 million converting our accounting functions over to a state-of-the-art software operation. I've spent the last 15+ years in the high technology manufacturing industry. I'm currently seeking a new CFO/Director of Finance opportunity here in Kansas City. (Be prepared to explain why?)*

The trick here is to prepare your commercial and to practice it several times every day in the mirror. The practice is designed to ensure you can deliver your message with enthusiasm, focus and clarity.

The only way you'll know is to watch yourself in the mirror. If there is no enthusiasm, do it until you're enthusiastic. Practice every day so that you're fully prepared.

Remember: There's no such thing as magic or luck here. You make your own luck every day. You just can't see it.

*Luck is when preparation meets opportunity.*

Opportunities are all around you. Either you didn't notice or you were unprepared or both. Now, you'll be more prepared for a real opportunity.

### What's your Search Focus?

Spend some quality time deciding what you're looking for - your Focus. Describe your ideal job.

Here are the components to creating a good Focus Statement:

- Title: Project Manager, Technical Analyst?

- Level: Entry, supervisor, manager, director, VP, C-level?

- Function: Sales, Marketing, Operations, Finance, Research?

- Type: Full-time, Part-time, Contract, Consulting?

- Industry: Aerospace, Defense, Automotive, Agriculture?

- Location: Open to relocation? How long a commute? Sales territory?

- Compensation: Range of desired pay? Other benefits?

- <u>Leadership or technical</u>: Lead people or manage things-accounts?

- <u>Target Companies</u>: List 10 companies you'd like to work for?

- <u>Deal Stoppers</u>: Like certain industries, 100% travel, foreign travel, exposure to danger, multi-level, sales, insurance, or work weekends?

### Can you have more than one Focus?

Sure, but be careful! Now, you've defused your time and effort in your search. We have no problem with a dual Focus. But, any more than that, we don't recommend.

# CHAPTER 5:
# ASSESSING YOUR CURRENT RESUME

*"Resume: a written exaggeration of only the good things a person has done in the past, as well as a wish list of the qualities a person would like to have." - Bo Bennett*

You've previously learned how *Positive Cash Flow (PCF)* and *Band Of Excellence (BOE)* relate to every employer on the planet. That's how your resume should read.

It must be abundantly clear to the reader what you've done previously to help your employer with his PCF/BOE goals. If not, why would any employer waste his time interviewing you? He wouldn't! A PCF/BOE rich resume is what gets you the phone call. From then on, speak PCF/BOE during both phone interviews and in person.

Scenario: I'll now take you through the exact process I took my last client through to create his compelling resume. His name was John Brown. Before I started, I asked John for a copy of his resume. I assumed that his resume was a Good resume, at least to him.

## *STEP 1*

Even though John had sixteen years of great experience, and just got his Master's degree in Architecture, his resume (below) was in bad shape.

---

John Brown

1111 Windsor Drive, Summit Mills, al 68654; 913.123.9876; bobo@gmail.com

Objective: to become an arkitect in a chalenging envirment

2004-Present: John's Home Improvement Company, al – Owner, made home repairs

2002-2004: Schmidt Construction, wa – Construction Superintindant, managed several project

1994-2002: Albertsons Food Store, ca - Asistant Store Manager, assisted store managr in running the store

Education: Bachelor and Master in Arkitecture from alabama U

Refrences:

Ted Brown: 213.345.221

Joe Smith: 213.436.278

Ralph Burns: 213.45.6657

---

I was stunned by the quality of his resume, especially the misspellings, but I offered no critique at first. My only goal was to move his resume from being Good to being Better. I just set it aside and began to ask John the following questions, while I took notes.

Without looking at your resume, record your answers to the following questions. then, compare your answers to your current resume and we'll see if there's a difference.

## *STEP 2*

Here are the questions I asked John.

### *Have you ever helped an Employer...?*

**Make more money by:**

- Selling more products or services?
- Bringing in new customers?
- Selling more to the same customers?
- Discovering new uses for an old product?
- Finding new ways to bring more money in the door?

**Save money by:**

- Consolidating?
- Eliminating?
- Getting a better price from a supplier?
- Being more efficient?
- Conserving?
- Saving time?

**Better use of what they already have by:**

- Streamlining?
- Process improvement?
- Reducing time required?
- Becoming more efficient or doing more with less?
- Better maintaining to extend service life?
- Finding a better, quicker, or easier way?

**Solve problems today to save $$$ tomorrow by:**

- Creating important policies and procedures?
- Creating better contracts?
- Managing risk better?
- Ensuring the right insurance is in force?
- Ensuring compliance with outside agencies?
- Creating better physical and cyber security procedures?
- Creating better property accountability procedures?
- Eliminating unsafe conditions?

**Meet or exceed the *Band Of Excellence?***

- What do you do (What function did it perform)?
- What *Band Of Excellence* did you have to meet or exceed?
- How did your Leader measure this?

**How did your work compare to others or to previous years?**

- How did your results compare to others?
- How did your results compare to previous years?
- Are you getting better over time?
- What did your Leader give you for being the best or for improving?
- What got better because you were there?

**What work experience are you most proud?**

- Brag a little!
- Make more money or save money?
- Better use what they already have?
- Solve problems today to save $$$ tomorrow?
- Achieve, sustain, or exceed your BOE?
- Most difficult task?
- Best results?

- Write down your story!

**Why are you leaving out the details?**

- How important was this task you're proud of?
- How many people were involved?

*How complicated was the task?*

- How much money was involved?
- Were you on a tight time deadline?
- With whom did you have to coordinate?
- Was there any risk of failure?
- If it wasn't easy, tell me why?
- Why're you so proud of this?

**Have you ever supervised the efforts of others?**

- How many?
- Who were they?
- What was the problem?
- What actions were taken by you or your team?
- What were the quantifiable results?

**How difficult was this task and why?**

- Don't leave out the details!
- How complex was the task?
- How big was the budget?
- What obstacles did you have to overcome?
- How difficult was it?
- Talk gross, total annual cost?
- How many people were involved (directly/indirectly)?
- What were the consequences of failure?

**Have you ever:**

- Led? Managed? Directed?
- Supervised?
- Coordinated?
- Facilitated?

**Why would anyone want to hire you?**

- What do you bring to the table?
- What would others say about you?
- Can you be counted on to produce excellent results?
- Don't leave out the details!

**What do you do best?**

- Received favorable comments?
- Receive praise?
- People came to you for advice or help?
- Received awards or special recognition?
- What're your special gifts?
- What gets you out of bed in the morning?

After asking these questions, I had two full pages of great material; even though I had to drag it out of John – kicking and screaming! I then asked John, why wasn't all this in your resume? He just stared at me with his mouth open. I again asked, why did you leave it out? Again, silence and a dumb look on his face.

*The sad truth is that most people have no clue how valuable they are to a potential employer.*

I then asked the killer question, *"John, how does this make you feel?"* He was obviously stunned by what had just happened. It took a while for it to sink in and he finally said, *"Wow! I had no idea all that should be in my resume."*

---

Still think your resume's great? This may help explain why you're not getting called for interviews. Your resume is just not compelling enough to generate the call.

## *What does "Compelling" mean?*

Think of your resume as a movie trailer. Is your movie trailer exciting enough to make someone want to see the movie? Is your resume compelling enough for someone to want to know more? Does your resume show your contributions to your Leader's PCF/BOE goals, the solutions and full range of skills you bring, or how your transferrable skills apply to any industry?

If not, then why would any employer in their right mind want to waste their time talking to you? Do a better job of selling your knowledge, skills, experience, achievements, attitude, and relationships than you've done in the past!

With the two full pages of notes I took from questioning John, I now had great *Positive Cash Flow* content that I could add to his Good resume to make it Better. However, my next goal was to take his resume from Better to Best.

Note: When building your resume, don't tell me what you were responsible for – no one cares! Instead, tell me what you, or your team, actually accomplished, finished, or made happen. What got better because you were there?

### *STEP 3*

---

*What follows in the next chapter is the exact process I used to produce the best compelling resume possible for John to make his phone ring more frequently.*

---

# CHAPTER 6:
# BUILDING YOUR COMPELLING RESUME

*"Do not be too timid and squeamish about your actions.*
*All life is an experiment."* - Ralph Waldo Emerson

Any Compelling Resume consists of these seven levels:

## *LEVEL 1: HEADING*

I started building John's new resume, from top to bottom, one level at a time.

John Brown

1111 Windsor Drive, Summit Mills, AL 68654; 913.123.9876; jbrown@gmail.com

If your email address is loverboy@xyz.com, go to Yahoo or Google and sign up for a free email address with your name only. You want to project a professional image. Details matter!

Boldface and enlarge your name to make it stand out. Use a phone number that you'll actually answer and change your voicemail to a more professional message, if necessary.

## *LEVEL 2: POSITION TITLES*

I asked John what position title he was seeking (right from his Focus Statement). He wanted to be a Design and Build Architect.

### Design and Build Architect

Most resumes have an Objective paragraph, which doesn't specifically state what you want to do. These titles come from your search Focus Statement. Clearly state what you want to do. Don't let the reader guess what you want to do.

## *LEVEL 3: KEY WORDS FOR SCANNING*

Since John had no clue what his key words might be, I did a quick web search for a generic job description of an Architect. Key words can also be assumed, if you know the industry. If you were the employer, what would you be seeking?

Ensure you own these key words because the employer will verify that you do. Keywords tend to be nouns that are industry-specific qualifications, skills, or terms. Some keywords include degrees or certifications, job titles, computer lingo, industry jargon, product names, company names and professional organizations. You can also identify keywords by visiting company websites and reviewing job postings.

Employers often search job banks looking for resumes with key words or requirements specific to their job description. Including more keywords throughout your online resume will increase your chances of being identified as a potential match. Also, use keywords in any description of yourself which most job sites require.

### *Be careful with Acronyms and Abbreviations:*

Every industry has their own unique set of jargon, acronyms, and abbreviations; the special language that only industry insiders understand. Unfortunately, not everyone reading your resume will understand them, especially if you're applying for positions outside your industry. A good rule is to always define your jargon, acronym, or abbreviation the first time it appears in any document.

As an example, in John's original resume he had ICF and SIP. In his final resume, you'll find Insulated Concrete Forms (ICF), and Structure Insulated Panel Systems (SIPS).

## How important is the Job Description?

There are two types of job descriptions; the generic job description from a web search to give you key words for adding to your resume and the employer's specific job description found in job postings (which is used for applying for posted positions and for interviewing). From searching the web for Architect Job Description, I found the following generic job description:

*Researches, plans, designs, and administers building projects for clients, applying knowledge of design, construction procedures, zoning and building codes, and building materials: Consults with client to determine functional and spatial requirements of new structure or renovation, and prepares information regarding design, specifications, materials, color, equipment, estimated costs, and construction time.*

*Plans layout of project and integrates engineering elements into unified design for client review and approval.*

*Prepares scale drawings and contract documents for building contractors. Represents client in obtaining bids and awarding construction contracts. Administers construction contracts and conducts periodic on-site observation of work during construction to monitor compliance with plans. May prepare operating and maintenance manuals, studies, and reports. May use computer-assisted design software and equipment to prepare project designs and plans. May direct activities of workers engaged in preparing drawings and specification documents.*

## Verify ownership of your Key Words:

My next step was to sit down with John and asked him which key words (bolded) from the above job description truthfully belonged to him. I told him that during the interview, the employer would attempt to verify if he truly owned those key words.

To prove that you own them you'll need some form of documentation (diploma, certificate, transcripts, and past performance reviews), or a great story to tell to convince them, or a personal reference from your past that can confirm your resume

John carefully selected about 30% of the key words from the job description. I then added them to John's key words, Level 3. In the end, these are the key words that John could easily substantiate.

This is what it looked like when I added it to his Compelling Resume:

Project / Project Manager / Plan / Design / Coordinate / Estimate Costs / Administer / Construction / Architecture / Architect / Engineer / Scale Drawings / Contracts / Client Review / Obtain Bid / Award Contract / Monitor Compliance / On-site Observation / CAD / Prepare Drawings / Zoning / Building Code

## LEVEL 4: MARKETING SUMMARY

At this point, I began to write John's compelling marketing summary. The purpose of this paragraph is to entice the reader to read the entire resume. I took the information from his resume (not much help) and from the two pages of notes I took earlier (as part of his resume assessment questions) and this is what I created.

*Career professional with a Master's degree in Architecture plus sixteen years of experience working with Albertson's, JE Dunn, Turner Construction, Walton, Raul Construction and as a business owner and entrepreneur. Key leadership roles in Food Store Management and the Residential and Commercial Construction industries.*

*Career Track: Professional growth as Assistant Store Manager, Construction Superintendent, Entrepreneur, and Home Improvement Business Owner.*

*Utilized principle centered leadership in managing multiple projects consisting of technical teams and subcontractors and developing partnerships and programs. Strong track record of increased responsibility, planning, designing, streamlining business processes, with excellent "word-of-mouth" customer satisfaction. Demonstrated entrepreneurial spirit that increased sales and profits.*

*Proven Record: Skilled at negotiating, estimating, budgeting, scheduling, monitoring compliance, on-site inspections, contracts, and conflict resolution. Consistently exceeded company standards for quality of work and completed requirements on-time, under budget, with excellent client reviews. Completed both a Bachelor's and Master's degree in Architecture at Alabama University concurrent with running his own home improvement business as an entrepreneur, taking 18-21 credit hours per semester.*

How many years of experience do you have? Within which industries have you worked? What were your job titles? This is just a snapshot.

Note: I added John's key words (underlined) in this level as well.

## *LEVEL 5: EDUCATION & TRAINING*

This level is straight forward. The only problem I had was clarifying what all his abbreviations meant to the common person; me.

### *Education and Special Training*

*Bachelor and Master's Degrees in Architecture from Alabama University, School of Architecture*

*Computer: Drafting (AutoCAD), Modeling (SketchUp, Revit), Graphics (Photoshop, Illustrator, Indesign), MS Office (Word, Outlook, Excel, and PowerPoint)*

*Construction: Carpentry (rough and finish), tile work, paint finishes, interior shading systems and floor plans for both spec and custom homes. Knowledgeable of building codes for AL, WA, and CA*

Note: I added more key words (underlined) above.

What special knowledge or training do you have that would make you stand out? Most resumes show education and special training last, which often gets overlooked. Here, John's education, computer and construction skills are listed separately and positioned in the middle of the resume (not at the end) to make it stand out more.

Note: The construction paragraph above actually summarizes John's experience and relates directly to architecture.

## *LEVEL 6: ACHIEVEMENTS AND SKILLS*

The information for this level again came from John's resume, my two pages of intake information and a list (below) of the most sought after transferrable skills on the planet.

These are the most sought after Transferrable Skills.

Led, Managed, Directed, Supervised, Coordinated, Facilitated, Administered, Created, Produced, Implemented, Communicated, Introduced, Presented, Planned, Trained, Designed, Engineered, Prepared, Reviewed, Streamlined, Estimated, Solved, Decided, Coached, Mentored, Inspired, Executed, Assessed, and Researched

Based on my 21 years of experience, these are the transferrable skills for which employers pay the most money. After I explained the list to John, I asked him, which transferrable skills do you own? Have you ever used these skills? From this list, he selected the following, which I added to Level 6:

*Led, Managed, Supervised, Coordinated, Inspired, Trained, Mentored, Streamlined, Communicated, Solved, Administered and Implemented.*

Then, I asked John if he could defend these transferrable skills and achievements with either some form of documentation (diploma, certificate, transcripts, and past performance reviews), or a great PAR story to tell to convince them, or a personal reference from his past that can confirm his skills.

With this information, I prepared to write his Selected Achievements and Skills, Level 6 adding his transferrable skills and key words.

### Selected Achievements and Skills

*Managed the successful completion of a $250,000, one-month, detailed, motorized shade installation project for the Ransom County, Taylor Museum of Contemporary Art. As a subcontractor with JE Dunn, coordinated with numerous stakeholders including museum owners, electricians, architects, and other subcontractors, completed the project ahead of schedule, under budget, with outstanding client reviews.*

*Led the efforts of 95 associates, as the Assistant Store Manager, for a $2.4 Million per month Albertson's Food Store in Sacramento, CA. Inspired team cohesion, improving performance and moral. Trained and mentored team members to enhance their professional development and improve customer service.*

*Supervised and conducted on-site inspections to monitor compliance which consistently saved money by getting the job done right the first time and eliminating costly rework. Streamlined procedures and operations to achieve more in the same amount of time.*

*Skills: Strong written and verbal communication skills. Personable and capable of working with all levels of management and technical leads. Proficient in problem solving, implementing complex solutions, scale drawings, contracts, obtaining bids and administering complex projects. Results and customer focused. International travel includes Korea, Malaysia, and Singapore.*

---

Note: I added more key words and transferrable skills above.

### Suggestions to develop your achievements:

Start each achievement with an action verb in the past tense (managed, led, and supervised). After the verb, tell your quantifiable results (with numbers!), include PCF/BOE related information, and include the details (PAR stories) that show how difficult it was to complete.

## *LEVEL 7: CAREER OVERVIEW*

The final level is a very important level even though it appears to be just a work history. It serves a valuable purpose; to diminish your liabilities. With a chronological resume, it's much easier to find flaws in your resume. The last ten years is what the employer needs to see. Going back more than 10 years may make you look too old.

*This format diminishes the adverse effects of several liabilities.*

It doesn't highlight liabilities like age, lack of career progression, most of your work experience in only one industry, or gaps in work. The content that precedes this level is so strong that any adverse effects are minimized. You're still providing the same information, but in a way to highlight your assets and diminish your liabilities.

### *Career Overview*

*Alabama University – Graduate Student, 2007-2011*

*John's Home Improvement Company, AL – Owner, 2004-Present*

*Schmidt Construction, WA – Construction Superintendent, 2002-2004*

*Albertson's Food Stores, CA - Assistant Store Manager, 1994-2002*

# *WHAT DOES A COMPELLING RESUME LOOK LIKE?*

## John Brown

1111 Windsor Drive, Summit Mills, AL 68654; 913.123.9876; jbrown@gmail.com

**Design and Build Architect**

Project / Project Manager / Plan / Design / Coordinate / Estimate Costs / Administer / Construction / Architecture / Architect / Engineer / Scale Drawings / Contracts / Client Review / Obtain Bid / Award Contract / Monitor Compliance / On-site Observation / CAD / Prepare Drawings / Zoning / Building Code

Career professional with a Master's degree in Architecture plus sixteen years of experience working with Albertson's, JE Dunn, Turner Construction, Walton, Raul Construction and as a business owner and entrepreneur. Key leadership roles in Food Store Management and the Residential and Commercial Construction industries.

Career Track: Professional growth as Assistant Store Manager, Construction Superintendent, Entrepreneur, and Home Improvement Business Owner.

Utilized principle centered leadership in managing multiple projects consisting of technical teams and subcontractors and developing partnerships and programs. Strong track record of increased responsibility, planning, designing, streamlining business processes, with excellent "word-of-mouth" customer satisfaction. Demonstrated entrepreneurial spirit that increased sales and profits.

Proven Record: Skilled at negotiating, estimating, budgeting, scheduling, monitoring compliance, on-site inspections, contracts, and conflict resolution. Consistently exceeded company standards for quality of work and completed requirements on-time, under budget, with excellent client reviews. Completed both a Bachelor's and Master's degree in Architecture at Alabama University concurrent with running his own home improvement business as an entrepreneur, taking 18-21 credit hours per semester.

### Education and Special Training:

**Bachelor and Master's Degrees in Architecture** from Alabama University, School of Architecture

**Computer:** Drafting (AutoCAD), Modeling (SketchUp, Revit), Graphics (Photoshop, Illustrator, Indesign), MS Office (Word, Outlook, Excel, and PowerPoint)

**Construction:** Carpentry (rough and finish), tile work, paint finishes, interior shading systems and floor plans for both spec and custom homes. Knowledgeable of building codes for AL, WA, and CA

### Selected Achievements and Skills:

- Managed the successfully completion of a $250,000, one-month, detailed, motorized shade installation project for the Ransom County, Taylor Museum of Contemporary Art. As a subcontractor with JE Dunn, coordinated with numerous stakeholders including museum owners, electricians, architects, and other subcontractors, completed the project ahead of schedule, under budget, with outstanding client reviews.

- Led the efforts of 95 associates, as the Assistant Store Manager, for a $2.4 Million per month Albertson's Food Store in Sacramento, CA. Inspired team cohesion, improving performance and moral. Trained and mentored team members to enhance their professional development and improve customer service.

- Supervised and conducted on-site inspections to monitor compliance which consistently saved money by getting the job done right the first time and eliminating costly rework. Streamlined procedures and operations to achieve more in the same amount of time.

Skills: Strong written and verbal communication skills. Personable and capable of working with all levels of management and technical leads. Proficient in problem solving, implementing complex solutions, scale drawings, contracts, obtaining bids and administering complex projects. Results and customer focused. International travel includes Korea, Malaysia, and Singapore.

### Career Overview:

Alabama University – Graduate Student, 2007-2011
John's Home Improvement Company, AL. – Owner, 2004-Present
Schmidt Construction, WA – Construction Superintendent, 2002-2004
Albertson's Food Stores, CA - Assistant Store Manager, 1994-2002

### Did this process strengthen your resume?

If you did STEPS 1-3, from Chapter 5, to the best of your ability, you should have two pages worth of details that will make a major difference to your resume and whether you receive a phone call. If not, go back and do it again – until you do. Use the same process to create your own Best Compelling Resume from top to bottom. Just make sure it speaks PCF/BOE.

## *BUILDING YOUR SPECIAL PURPOSE RESUMES*

Now that you've finished your Best Compelling Resume, there are still a few things left to do:

- First, don't forget to do a final spell check of your resume. Your computer will tell you that you have sentence fragments – that's okay! Just make sure everything is spelled correctly. Remember to delete all articles (a, an & the).

- Second, have someone proof read your resume to ensure it makes sense and all jargon, acronyms and abbreviations are defined the first time they appear.

- Third, check your resume for any exaggerations, opinions, and superlatives, that can't be supported. This could cause you not to get a phone call. So, be careful! Just state the facts (not your opinion) and let the interviewer decide how good you are.

- Finally, it's time to convert your Compelling Resume into three Special Purpose Resumes; a Face-to-face Networking Resume (to hand-carry, hardcopy), an Advertised Job Resume (only used to apply for advertised positions found in the paper or on the web), and a Web Resume (for Job Banks and Social Networking Sites).

### *Face-to-Face Networking Resume*

Your Face-to-Face Networking Resume, a paper/hardcopy version, is the same as the Compelling Resume except that the Level 3 (key words) section is deleted, because it's not needed. However, it is no more than one page in length. This resume is designed to be hand delivered to others at advice meetings, visits, when meeting someone for lunch, Job Fairs, and any other opportunity to network.

### Advertised Job Resume

This version of your resume is used when applying for advertised positions that you find in the newspaper, trade magazines, or on the web. This resume is the same as your Compelling Resume except that the Level 2 (position titles) is deleted, because they don't apply.

### Web Resume

Anytime you post your resume on the web (Job Banks, Social Networking Sites, Monster.com, CareerBuilder.com, etc.), convert your Compelling Resume into a Plain Text document. Length here is not an issue. Some sites accept Word docs; however, many won't recognize specialized text, bullets, tabs, boldface or formatted text. Your resumes, unless converted, run the risk of showing up on an interviewer's computer screen as gibberish. You can avoid formatting issues by saving it as a Text Only/Plain Text document.

After you've saved it, open your resume and this is what you should see:

---

John Brown

111 Wind Drive, Summit Mills, AL 68654; 913.123.9876; jbrown@gmail.com

Design and Build Architect

Project / Project Manager / Plan / Design / Coordinate / Estimate Costs / Administer / Construction / Architecture / Architect / Engineer / Scale Drawings / Contract Documents / Client Review / Obtain Bid / Award Contract / Monitor Compliance / On-site Observation / CAD / Prepare Report / Zoning / Building Code

---

Now, separate the major sections of your resume with the space bar and capitalize the major headings and resave it in Text Only/Plain Text document. This is what you should see;

---

JOHN BROWN

111 Wind Drive, Summit Mills, AL 68654

913.123.9876

jbrown@gmail.com

DESIGN AND BUILD ARCHITECT

Project / Project Manager / Plan / Design / Coordinate / Estimate Costs / Administer / Construction / Architecture / Architect / Engineer / Scale Drawings / Contract Documents / Client Review / Obtain Bid / Award Contract / Monitor Compliance / On-site Observation / CAD / Prepare Report / Zoning / Building Code

---

Notice how re-spacing and capitalizing makes your resume more readable. Once posted, again re-space and capitalize so it's readable. When finished, email it to yourself - so you can see what it looks like.

Then, go back and make any final edits to ensure it looks the way you want it to look on the web site.

Now you have a resume you can post on Facebook in the About me box, and on LinkedIn.com. These special purpose resumes have produced considerably more phone calls for my clients because now the employer can clearly see the skills, talents, and abilities they can contributed to their PCF/BOE related achievements.

*Did this help you strengthen your resume? Do you now have a better understanding of how to write and speak in the language every employer understands?*

## THE END!

*Congratulations!* You've reached the end of this book. Thank you for reading! Please remember to share what you have learned with others. If you help others succeed, they'll return the favor.

This book focused on creating a compelling resume strong enough to make your phone ring. However, if you have additional concerns, these books, also available from all online book retailers, will help you:

- *Interview Like You Mean It:* How to interview strong enough to receive a job offer.

- *Negotiating Total Compensation:* How to negotiate strong enough to receive the highest offer the employer can afford.

- *19+ Proven Ways to Get Your Resume to the Right People.*

- *Changing Your Career?* How to change careers (like those leaving the US Military).

If you found this book of value, you'll also find value in the other books from *The Effectiveness Guide* series (see Other Books).

The subjects covered will enhance your career by teaching you how to become absolutely essential to any organization and how to become more effective tomorrow than you are today.

*You can do this! I have faith in you. What's holding you back?*

### Self-Assessment:

After reading this book:

- How can you use what you've learned to become more effective tomorrow than you are today?

- How can you use it to become absolutely essential and irreplaceable to any employer?

- How can you use it outside of work (in your community, church, or home) to become better?

- Who else could use it to help them become better?

*Do something meaningful with your life. Pay it forward. Help someone else rise.*

# ACKNOWLEDGEMENTS

*"Many people will walk in and out of your life, but only true friends will leave footprints in your heart."*
*- Eleanor Roosevelt*

I'd like to recognize those with whom I've had the pleasure of serving, whose Leadership and Character I vividly recall, many of whom are not here today to tell their story.

For my military career, I thank Betty McInte, Edward J. Murphy (my Dad), Dale R. Nelson, Geoffrey "Jeff" Prosch, Craig "Randy" Rutler, Dave Wagner, John Andrews, John "The Bear" Warren, John "Jack" Costello, Dan Labin, and Ron Nicholl for their example of Effective Leadership.

*To my fellow Brothers and Sisters-in-Arms, I thank you for your faithful service to our nation, especially those who have fallen in the line-of-duty.*

Special thanks to my long-time mentor and friend, Joyce Kuntz, who encouraged me to write this book. After leaving the US Military, Joyce was my first and best employer when I joined her consulting firm in Seattle years ago. Joyce is gone now, but her legacy lives on in this book.

*"I must be able to say with sincerity that to see things differently is a strength, not a weakness, in my relationship with others."*
*- Joyce Kuntz*

I thank Joyce's husband, Ed Kuntz, who turned out to be the man who brought me to Seattle from Kansas City, to start my incredible second career as an Executive Coach.

For my coaching career, I thank Tony Robbins, Bernard Haldane, Jack Bissell, Len Drew, Wayne McCullum, Bob Schrier, John Hurtig, and Bob Gerberg for their mentoring and coaching.

I thank my Nephew, Rob Chase, for creating the superb cover graphics and his sound advice along the way.

I thank my editors, Adriane Hesselbein, Terri Beard, Lance Revo, Dan Labin, Dennis Cavin, Bill O'Donnell, Andrew Potter, and Kevin Hughes, who did a great job helping me make this book more understandable and useful.

A special thanks to my two dear friends, partners, and co-authors, Lee Lacy and Jason Bowne, who continue to support me in this worthwhile effort.

For all those whose names are not found here, rest assured that you are not forgotten. Your legacy lives on in my heart and in this book because of your immeasurable contributions to my life. This book is for you.

And, finally, I thank my soul-mate and wife, *Diana*, for her love, encouragement and understanding throughout this process.

*When I count my blessings, I always count her twice.*

# ABOUT THE FOUNDER

*"I expect to pass through this world but once; any good thing therefore that I can do, or any kindness that I can show to any fellow creature, let me do it now; let me not defer or neglect it, for I shall not pass this way again."* - Stephan Grelle

I was lucky! From age 7, I knew what I wanted to be when I grew up. I wanted to be a Soldier. In 1964, four days after graduating from High School, I joined the US Army and found myself in Basic Training and Advanced Infantry Training at Fort Dix, New Jersey.

A year later, I became a Cadet at the United States Military Academy at West Point. In 1970, I graduated as a 2d Lieutenant headed to Airborne and Ranger School, then off to Viet Nam for a year.

In 1978, I returned to West Point to teach Military Science and earned my Master's Degree from Long Island University in night school. My greatest achievement during my time in the military was helping 1400 soldiers begin their college education during my last two years in West Germany as a Battalion Commander.

I wanted to give my soldiers something of real value - something that no one could ever take away. After 23 years as a US Army Officer, from Viet Nam to Desert Storm, I retired in 1993.

I then decided, with a little help from Anthony Robbins, that my second career would be as an Executive Coach. For 21 years, I worked for four of the largest consulting, outplacement and e-cruiting companies in America from Seattle, San Diego, to Kansas City. I helped hundreds of people, from recent college graduates to CEO's, to find and build the careers they were meant to have.

In 2012, I retired a second time and decided to document everything I learned from those I admired and willingly followed for the past 44 years in both the US Military as an Army Officer and in Corporate America as an Executive Coach. Since many of them aren't here today to tell their stories, I wanted to pay tribute to them before their lessons were lost forever. Thanks to them, I have collected thousands of small and simple things (tactics, techniques, and tools) that you'll need to know to assist you throughout your career.

In 2014, I created TheCAREERMaker.com, a site dedicated to providing you with the best-in-class wisdom, knowledge, and advice on how to maximize your true career potential by teaching three simple things; how to become absolutely essential and irreplaceable to any leader, how to become more effective tomorrow than you are today, and how to find and build the career you were meant to have. My greatest joy comes from helping others avoid or overcome the problems I've faced during my lifetime.

In 2016, with the help of my two partners and co-authors *Lee O. Lacy* and *Jason Bowne*, I finally completed The Effectiveness Guide, which teaches others how to maximize their true career potential by consistently produce excellent results; treating others with dignity, respect, and kindness; and how to identify, measure, and enhance their *value added* to their career, company, team, community, and family.

Today, I'm fortunate to get to live in Phoenix, AZ, where I enjoy writing, eating sushi, genealogy, and watching movies with family, friends, and my best friend - my wife, *Diana*.

# OTHER BOOKS

## THESE BOOKS WILL TEACH YOU HOW TO MAXIMIZE YOUR TRUE CAREER POTENTIAL.

## AVAILABLE FROM ALL MAJOR ONLINE BOOK RETAILERS.

If you liked this volume, you'll really like the others in our collection.
To view all our books in our Book Store, *@TheCareerMaker.com.*

**From** *The Effectiveness Guide* **series, topics include:**

Volume 1: Lead People and Manage Everything Else

Volume 2: Your Guide to Better Delegating

Volume 3: Your Guide to Better Planning

Volume 4: Your Guide to Better Organizing

Volume 5: Your Guide to Better Communicating

Volume 6: Your Guide to Better Problem Solving & Decision Making

Volume 7: Your Guide to Better Awareness

Volume 8: Your Guide to Better Training

Volume 9: Your Guide to Better Motivating

Volume 10: Your Guide to Better Character

Volume 11: The Effectiveness Guide *(includes Volumes 1-10)*

Volume 12: Your Guide to Better Followership

Volume 13: Make it Happen! Why Everything in Life is a Project

Volume 14: Your Guide to Better Credibility

**From *The Career Potential* series, topics include:**

Volume 1: Finding a New Job in 90 Days or Less

Volume 2: Choosing a Career That Matters

Volume 3: Interview Like You Mean It

Volume 4: Does Your Resume Make Your Phone Ring?

Volume 5: Negotiating Total Compensation

Volume 6: 19+ Proven Ways to Get Your Resume to the Right People

Volume 7: Changing Your Career?

Volume 8: Getting THE Call

To view all our books in our Book Store, *@TheCareerMaker.com*..

## ONE LAST THING...

Finally, if you feel this information could help someone else, please take a few moments to let them know. If it turns out to make a difference in their life, they'll be forever grateful to you – as will I.

*Let's make a difference together – one person at a time!*

All the best!

Ed

Founder of TheCAREERMaker.com
*email: ed.murphy77@gmail.com*

*Stop wishing you were better and do something about it today!*

# WANT TO STAND OUT?

**See how at *TheCareerMaker.com***

# INDEX

Made in the USA
Middletown, DE
29 September 2017